THE LITTLE
FISH

COOKBOOK

THE LITTLE
FISH
COOKBOOK

ACROPOLIS BOOKS

First published by Ultimate Editions in 1996

© 1996 Anness Publishing Limited

Ultimate Editions is an imprint of
Anness Publishing Limited
1 Boundary Row
London SE1 8HP

This edition distributed in Canada by
Book Express, an imprint of
Raincoast Books Distribution Limited

ISBN 1 86035 190 5

Publisher Joanna Lorenz
Senior Cookery Editor Linda Fraser
Assistant Editor Emma Brown
Designers Patrick McLeavey & Jo Brewer
Illustrator Anna Koska
Photographers James Duncan, Amanda Heywood,
Karl Adamson, Steve Baxter & Michelle Garrett
Recipes Carla Capalbo, Steven Wheeler, Christine
France, Carole Clements, Elizabeth Wolf-Cohen,
Hilaire Walden, Sarah Gates, Alex Barker, Liz Trigg,
Shirley Gill & Laura Washburn

For all recipes, quantities are given in both metric and
imperial measures, and, where appropriate, measures are also
given in standard cups and spoons. Follow one set, but not a
mixture, because they are not interchangeable.

Printed in Singapore by
Star Standard Industries Pte Ltd

Contents

Introduction

Frequently described as the perfect food, fish is packed with protein, has very little carbohydrate and is a good source of vitamins and minerals. White fish, like cod or haddock, is extremely low in fat, while the fat in oilier varieties, like mackerel and herring, is polyunsaturated and highly beneficial because the fatty acids in these fish are believed to play a part in preventing coronary heart disease. If we eat the bones, as we do when we tuck into a portion of deep-fried whitebait or canned pilchards, we obtain calcium.

Although healthy eating is a persuasive argument for enjoying fish, it is only one of a raft of reasons. Fish is the ultimate fast food. It is generally sold prepared, needs very little cooking and, because it has less connective tissue than meat, there is very little shrinkage. It is versatile, lending itself to a wide range of cooking methods, such as poaching, steaming, grilling, frying, braising, baking, roasting and even barbecuing. Because of the high moisture content, it is an ideal candidate for the microwave, rewarding the careful cook with maximum flavour. Try it sauced or in salads, with pasta or as the basis for a risotto or pilaff. Stick it on skewers, toss it in a wok with crisp-tender vegetables, try it wrapped in spinach or packaged in paper. Make it into a pie, a pasty or a pâté, or enjoy it served simply with a squeeze of lemon juice and grinding of black pepper.

Explore the wealth of different types of fish and shellfish – over sixty varieties in Britain alone. Tap into your fishmonger's fund of knowledge. Ask him or her for recommendations and advice on cooking methods. A good fishmonger, given a considerate amount of notice, will gladly obtain a special type of fish, and will also prepare it in an appropriate manner for a specific recipe.

Choose your fishmonger as carefully as you do your butcher and you shouldn't ever have cause to question the quality of the merchandise. Even so, it is useful to know what to look for when choosing fish. The eyes of whole fish should be clear and bright; the skin shiny and colourful. It is sometimes suggested that fresh fish should have no odour, but this is not true: it should have a fresh sea smell; any hint of ammonia (except with skate, which may have a very faint whiff, which will disappear on blanching) and you should certainly not buy. Fish fillets should have a neat shape; the flesh of white fish should be translucent. If smoked, the fish should have a pleasant smoky aroma and good colour. Bright yellow smoked haddock fillets are not naturally that colour; they are dyed.

Fish and shellfish (with the occasional exception of octopus) is never tough, but if it is overcooked, the flesh will be dry and tasteless, and nutrients will have been lost. Fish is ready as soon as the protein coagulates. The general advice is to test the fish with the point of a sharp knife; if it flakes easily, it is cooked.

We've trawled the world for the finest fish recipes, from Maryland Crab Cakes to Moroccan Fish Tagine. Within these pages you'll find everything from soups to salads – an irresistible invitation to eat more fish.

Familiar Fish & Shellfish

COD

This popular white fish has firm flaky flesh and good flavour. It is good grilled, fried, baked and skewered. Members of the cod family include haddock, hake, coley, ling, pollock and whiting.

CRAB

The meat from this shellfish is of two sorts. Brown meat from inside the hard upper shell is soft and rich, whereas the white meat found in the claws and body is more dense and sweet. Crabs are often sold cooked; choose one that is heavy for its size.

DOVER SOLE

This has long been a favourite, thanks to its delicate flavour and fine white flesh. It is frequently fried or grilled whole.

LOBSTER

The meat of this large crustacean has an exquisite flavour. For best results, buy live lobsters when possible.

MACKEREL

An oily fish that is particularly good grilled or barbecued, mackerel needs a sharp sauce to counteract its rich flavour.

MONKFISH

Ugly to look at but delicious to eat, monkfish has firm, meaty flesh with a flavour reminiscent of lobster.

MUSSELS

Available all year round, mussels have a wonderful, sweet flavour and can be eaten steamed, baked with a stuffing, or added to sauces and salads.

SALMON

Deservedly held in high regard, the fresh fish has firm flesh with wonderful flavour. Farmed salmon is widely available but the wild fish has an even better flavour. It can be cooked by most methods and is truly delectable poached, baked or barbecued whole. It is also excellent smoked.

SARDINES

Sardines should be eaten very fresh, or cooked from frozen. They can be grilled, barbecued or baked. Canned sardines are a very good store cupboard standby and can be used for a tasty pizza topping.

SCALLOPS

The edible part of the scallop is the round white muscle and the orange, pointed coral, or roe. These tender shellfish are rich yet delicately flavoured.

SKATE

Related to the shark, skate is a delicately flavoured fish with a cartilaginous skeleton. Usually fried in butter, it can also be grilled or barbecued.

TROUT

More often farmed than wild, trout makes very good gravadlax and is also delicious fried, grilled or smoked.

TUNA

A very large meaty fish, often eaten rare, fresh tuna has a robust flavour. Canned tuna tastes more mellow, and is popular for salads and sauces.

TURBOT

Usually sold as steaks or fillets, turbot is an expensive treat. It has an excellent flavour and is widely considered to be the finest of the flat fish.

Techniques

FILLETING A ROUND FISH

Cut off the head. With the tip of a knife, cut through the skin all along the length of the backbone. Working from head to tail, use short strokes to cut one fillet off the rib bones in one piece. Cut across the tail to release the fillet. Repeat for the other fillet.

FILLETING A FLAT FISH

Make an incision in the skin around the head, then cut down the centre of one side of the fish. Working from the head end, and from the centre outwards, scrape the flesh off the bones to ease the first fillet away in one piece. Repeat with the remaining three fillets.

SKINNING A WHOLE FLAT FISH

Lay the fish on a flat surface and cut through the skin just above the tail. Ease enough skin away to get a grip, then pull it off. Repeat on the second side. To get a firm grip, you may find it helpful to salt your fingers.

SKINNING A FISH FILLET

Lay the fillet flat, skin-side down, tail end towards you. Cut across the tail end, through to the skin. Grip the bit of skin and insert the knife blade so it is almost parallel to the skin. Cut the fillet away using a sawing motion.

PEELING PRAWNS

Pull off the head, slit or pull the shell apart along the underside between the legs, then use your thumbs to slip it off and release the tail. Straighten the prawn, then carefully pull out the vein from the head end. If it breaks off, use a sharp knife to make a small cut down the back to remove the rest. Rinse and pat dry.

CLEANING MUSSELS OR CLAMS

Discard any shellfish with cracked or broken shells; also any shells which are not tightly closed or which do not snap shut when tapped. Scrub the shells and remove the hairy 'beard' which sticks out from the shell. Rinse under running water. If you have harvested the shellfish yourself, leave them in a large bucket of sea water for several hours, changing the water once or twice, so that they expel any sand. For clams, add a handful or two of cornmeal or flour to the water to help the cleansing process.

SCALING FISH

Holding the fish by the tail under running water over a clean sink, scrape off the scales with a blunt knife. Work from the tail towards the head.

11

COOK'S TIPS

• *To calculate how much fish to buy, the rule of thumb is to allow about 150-175g/5-6oz fish fillets or 175-200g/6-7oz fish steaks per person.*

• *Different types of fish can be mixed in soups and stews to create sensational flavours. Try a mixture of white fish with smoked fish fillets and prawns.*

• *When poaching whole fish, start with cold water to preserve the shape of the skin; add fillets or steaks to simmering liquid.*

Starters

Prawn & Corn Bisque

INGREDIENTS

30ml/2 tbsp olive oil
1 onion, finely chopped
50g/2oz/¼ cup butter or margarine
25g/1oz/¼ cup plain flour
750ml/1¼ pints/3⅔ cups fish or
chicken stock, or clam juice
250ml/8fl oz/1 cup milk
175g/6oz cooked prawns, shelled, plus 4 whole
prawns to garnish
250g/9oz/1½ cups sweetcorn
(fresh, frozen or canned)
2.5ml/½ tsp finely chopped fresh dill or thyme
pinch of salt
dash of Tabasco sauce
120ml/4fl oz/½ cup single cream
dill sprigs, to garnish

SERVES 4

1 Heat the oil in a large heavy-based saucepan. Add the chopped onion and fry over a low heat for 8–10 minutes, until softened.

2 Meanwhile melt the butter or margarine in a separate saucepan. Whisk in the flour and cook for 1 minute, then gradually pour in the stock or clam juice and milk, whisking until the sauce boils and thickens. Lower the heat and simmer for about 5–8 minutes, stirring frequently.

3 Add the prawns to the onion with the sweetcorn and dill or thyme. Cook for 2–3 minutes over a gentle heat, stirring, then add the sauce, mixing well. Purée 750ml/1¼ pints/3⅔ cups of the bisque in a blender or food processor, return it to the pan and stir well. Add salt and Tabasco to taste.

4 Stir in the cream. Heat the bisque gently, stirring occasionally until warmed through. Do not allow it to approach boiling point. Serve in heated bowls, garnished with dill sprigs and prawns.

13

Blinis with Smoked Salmon & Dill

1 Heat the milk with 15g/½oz/1 tbsp of the butter in a saucepan, stirring, until the butter has melted. Pour into a jug and cool to hand-hot.

2 Mix the buckwheat flour, plain flour, salt and yeast in a large bowl. Separate one of the eggs. Make a well in the centre of the dry ingredients and add the milk mixture, the whole egg and the extra yolk. Beat to a smooth batter. Cover with clear film and leave to rise in a warm place for 1–2 hours.

3 Whisk the egg white in a bowl until stiff peaks form. Fold it into the batter. Heat a heavy-based frying pan or griddle and grease with some of the remaining butter. Drop tablespoons of the batter on to the pan, spacing them well apart. Cook for 40 seconds, until bubbles appear on the surface.

INGREDIENTS

350ml/12fl oz/1½ cups milk
25g/1oz/2 tbsp butter
115g/4oz/1 cup buckwheat flour
115g/4oz/1 cup plain flour
pinch of salt
15ml/1 tbsp easy-blend dried yeast
2 eggs
150ml/¼ pint/⅔ cup crème fraîche
45ml/3 tbsp chopped fresh dill
225g/8oz smoked salmon, thinly sliced
dill sprigs, to garnish

SERVES 4

4 Flip over the blinis and cook for 30 seconds on the other side. Wrap in foil and keep hot while cooking the rest of the blinis, buttering the pan each time.

5 Mix the crème fraîche and dill in a bowl. Serve the blinis topped with the smoked salmon and dill cream. Garnish with dill sprigs.

Crab & Ricotta Tartlets

INGREDIENTS

225g/8oz/2 cups plain flour
pinch of salt
115g/4oz/½ cup butter, diced
225g/8oz/1 cup ricotta cheese
15ml/1 tbsp grated onion
30ml/2 tbsp freshly grated Parmesan cheese
2.5ml/½ tsp mustard powder
2 eggs, plus 1 egg yolk
225g/8oz crabmeat
30ml/2 tbsp chopped fresh parsley
2.5-5ml/½-1 tsp anchovy essence
5-10 ml/1-2 tsp lemon juice
salt and cayenne pepper
salad leaves, to garnish

SERVES 4

1 Preheat the oven to 200°C/400°F/Gas 6. Sift the flour and salt into a bowl, and rub in the butter until the mixture resembles fine breadcrumbs. Stir in about 60ml/4 tbsp cold water and mix to make a firm dough.

2 Turn the dough on to a floured worksurface and knead lightly, then roll out and use to line four 10cm/4in tartlet tins. Prick the bases with a fork, line with greaseproof paper and fill with baking beans. Chill for 30 minutes.

3 Bake the pastry cases for 10 minutes, then remove the greaseproof paper and beans and bake for a further 10 minutes.

4 Meanwhile, beat the ricotta cheese, grated onion, Parmesan cheese and mustard powder together until they become soft. Gradually beat in the eggs and egg yolk, then gently stir in the crabmeat and chopped parsley. Add the anchovy essence, lemon juice, salt and cayenne pepper, to taste.

5 Remove the four tartlet tins from the oven and turn down the temperature to 180°C/350°F/Gas 4. Spoon the filling into the tins and bake for 20 minutes, until set and golden brown. Serve hot with a garnish of salad leaves.

15

Ceviche

INGREDIENTS

350g/12oz cooked king prawns, plus 2 extra
to garnish
350g/12oz scallops, shelled, with corals intact
2 tomatoes
1 mango, about 175g/6oz
1 red onion, finely chopped
350g/12oz salmon fillet
1 red chilli
juice of 8 limes
30ml/2 tbsp caster sugar
2 pink grapefruit
3 oranges
5 limes
salt and ground black pepper

SERVES 6

2 Skin the salmon and cut into small pieces, discarding any bones. Slice the chilli in half and discard the seeds. Chop finely and add to the mixing bowl. Add the salmon, lime juice and sugar. Mix gently, cover and leave to marinate for 3 hours.

3 Peel and segment all the citrus fruits, except for 1 lime. Drain well and mix with the fish. Season and garnish with prawns and the reserved lime, halved.

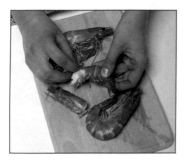

1 Peel and devein the king prawns and discard the shells. Using a sharp knife, cut the scallops into 1cm/½in square pieces. Dice the tomatoes and the mango. Place the prawns, scallops, diced tomatoes and mango in a large mixing bowl. Add the chopped red onion and mix together well.

Grilled Mussels with Cumin

INGREDIENTS

25g/ 1oz/ 2 tbsp butter, softened
1 garlic clove, crushed
pinch of ground cumin
45ml/ 3 tbsp chopped fresh parsley
45ml/ 3 tbsp chopped fresh coriander
25g/ 1oz/ 3 tbsp fresh brown breadcrumbs
12 green mussels or 24 small mussels,
on the half shell
ground black pepper
parsley or coriander sprigs, to garnish

SERVES 4

1 Using a wooden spoon, beat the softened butter with the crushed garlic in a bowl. Add the cumin and the chopped herbs and mix well. Stir in the fresh brown breadcrumbs, with a generous grinding of black pepper and mix well to combine. Preheat the grill.

2 Spoon a little of the breadcrumb mixture on to each mussel. Place on a rack over the grill pan and grill for 2 minutes. Garnish with sprigs of parsley or coriander and serve.

COOK'S TIP

To chop the fresh herbs, either use a mezzaluna (a curved blade with a handle at either end) or simply put the parsley and coriander in a straight-sided mug and snip them repeatedly with sharp kitchen scissors.

17

Maryland Crab Cakes with Tartare Sauce

INGREDIENTS

675g/ 1½lb fresh crabmeat
1 egg, beaten
30ml/ 2 tbsp mayonnaise
15ml/ 1 tbsp Worcestershire sauce
15ml/ 1 tbsp dry sherry
30ml/ 2 tbsp chopped fresh parsley
15ml/ 1 tbsp snipped chives or dill
45ml/ 3 tbsp olive oil
salt and ground black pepper
chives, salad leaves and lemon halves, to garnish
TARTARE SAUCE
1 egg yolk
15ml/ 1 tbsp white wine vinegar
30ml/ 2 tbsp Dijon mustard
250ml/ 8fl oz corn or peanut oil
30ml/ 2 tbsp lemon juice
2 spring onions, finely chopped
30ml/ 2 tbsp chopped drained capers
2 dill pickles, finely chopped
45ml/ 3 tbsp chopped fresh parsley

SERVES 4

1 Pick over the crabmeat, removing any shell or cartilage, keeping the pieces of crabmeat as large as possible. In a mixing bowl, combine the beaten egg with the mayonnaise, Worcestershire sauce, sherry and herbs. Season with salt and pepper, then gently fold in the crabmeat.

2 Divide the mixture into eight and gently form each portion into an oval cake. Place between greaseproof paper on a baking sheet. Chill for at least 1 hour.

3 Meanwhile make the sauce. Whisk the egg yolk in a bowl until smooth. Add the vinegar and mustard, with a little salt and pepper, and whisk briefly to blend. Whisking constantly, add the oil in a slow steady stream until the mixture thickens. Add the remaining ingredients, mixing well. Check the seasoning, cover and chill.

4 Preheat the grill. Brush a baking sheet with a little of the olive oil. Carefully transfer the crab cakes to the baking sheet, then brush them with the remaining oil. Grill the crab cakes, about 15cm/6in from the heat, for about 5 minutes on each side. Serve at once, with the tartare sauce, garnished with chives, salad leaves and lemon halves.

Gravadlax Trout

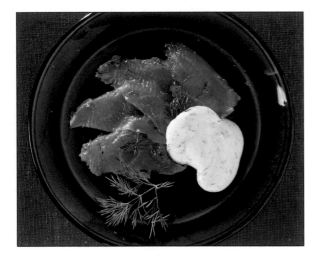

INGREDIENTS

2 large trout, cleaned, heads removed
1 bunch dill
seasonings (see method for quantities): coarse
salt, caster sugar and
black peppercorns, crushed
MUSTARD SAUCE
5ml/ 1 tsp dry mustard
15ml/ 1 tbsp chopped fresh dill
10ml/ 2 tsp caster sugar
5ml/ 1 tsp cider vinegar
75ml/ 5 tbsp soured cream

SERVES 4

1 Slit each trout from belly to tail in a straight line, open out and place belly-down on a surface. Press firmly along the backbone, down to the tail. Turn over and use the point of a knife to ease out the backbone in one piece. Pick out any stray bones.

2 Weigh the trout. For every 450g/1lb you need 7.5ml/1½ tsp each of the seasonings. Place one of the trout in a non-metallic dish, skin side down. Reserve four dill sprigs for the garnish and spread the rest on top of the trout to cover it completely.

3 Mix the seasonings and sprinkle evenly over the dill. Top it with the other trout, skin side up, cover with foil or a plate and add weights to compress the fish.

4 Chill for 48 hours, turning every 6–12 hours and basting with the brine which forms in the dish. Mix all the sauce ingredients together in a bowl, cover and chill.

5 Remove the dill and seasoning from the fish and pat dry. Cut the trout into fillets, or slice horizontally. Fan out the slices, garnish with the reserved dill sprigs and serve with the mustard sauce.

Smoked Salmon Pâté

INGREDIENTS

350g/12oz thinly sliced smoked salmon
150ml/¼ pint/⅔ cup double cream
finely grated rind and juice of 1 lemon
salt and ground black pepper
dill sprigs, to garnish
Melba toast, to serve

SERVES 4

1 Line four small ramekins with clear film. Using a sharp knife, cut the smoked salmon into strips, making sure that the strips are long enough to line the ramekins  and overlap the edges. Fit the strips neatly into the ramekins so that there are no gaps.

2 Process the rest of the smoked salmon with the double cream and the lemon rind and juice in a food processor or blender until it comes together to give a thick consistency. Scrape the mixture into a bowl. Taste and add salt and pepper, with more lemon juice, if liked.

3 Pack the lined ramekins with the smoked salmon pâté, then wrap the loose strips of salmon neatly over the top of each ramekin. Cover and chill for at  least 30 minutes before turning out the pâtés on to individual plates. Garnish each plate with dill sprigs and serve with Melba toast.

21

Lunch & Supper Dishes

Stuffed Sardines

INGREDIENTS

900g/ 2lb fresh sardines, cleaned
60ml/ 4 tbsp olive oil
75g/ 3oz/ 1 cup wholemeal breadcrumbs
1 onion, finely chopped
50g/ 2oz/ 1/3 cup sultanas
50g/ 2oz/ 1/2 cup pine nuts
50g/ 2oz can anchovy fillets, drained
60ml/ 4 tbsp chopped fresh parsley
salt and ground black pepper
banana leaves, to serve (optional)

SERVES 4

1 Preheat the oven to 200°C/400°F/ Gas 6. Rinse the sardines and dry them thoroughly with kitchen paper. Heat 30ml/2 tbsp of the oil in a frying pan and fry the breadcrumbs until golden. Using a slotted spoon, transfer the breadcrumbs to a bowl.

2 Heat half the remaining oil in the frying pan, add the onion and fry until golden. Stir in the sultanas, pine nuts, anchovies and parsley. Stir in the breadcrumbs, mix well and add salt and pepper to taste.

3 Stuff each of the cleaned sardines with the anchovy stuffing mixture, taking care to close the cavities firmly. Use a spoon to do this, or your hands if you find it easier. Arrange the sardines close together in a single layer in a shallow ovenproof dish. Scatter any remaining filling over the top of the fish.

4 Drizzle the remaining oil over the sardines. Bake for 30 minutes until tender, then serve on banana leaves, if you like.

Poached Skate & Black Butter

INGREDIENTS

1 litre / 1¾ pints / 4 cups water
1 carrot, sliced
1 small onion, sliced
1 bouquet garni
5ml / 1 tsp salt
6 peppercorns
120ml / 4fl oz / ½ cup white wine vinegar
8 skate wings
fresh herbs, to garnish
BLACK BUTTER
115g / 4oz / ½ cup butter
30ml / 2 tbsp drained capers

SERVES 4

1 Place the water with the carrot, onion, bouquet garni, salt and peppercorns in a large saucepan. Add 75ml/5 tbsp of the wine vinegar. Bring to the boil, lower the heat and simmer, uncovered, for 20 minutes. Strain the liquid (court bouillon) into a jug, discarding the flavouring ingredients.

2 Rinse the skate wings and dry them on kitchen paper. Put them in a large shallow pan and cover with the court bouillon. Bring to simmering point and poach for 10–12 minutes or until cooked. Drain, place on a large platter and keep hot.

3 Heat the butter in a pan; as soon as it turns a rich brown, remove it from the heat. Stir in the capers. Pour the butter over the skate. Add the remaining vinegar to the pan and heat through quickly, swirling it around. Pour the vinegar over the fish and serve at once, garnished with herbs.

24

Steamed Chilli Mussels

INGREDIENTS

2 red chillies
6 ripe tomatoes
30ml/ 2 tbsp peanut oil
2 garlic cloves, crushed
2 shallots, finely chopped
1.2kg/ 2½lb fresh mussels
30ml/ 2 tbsp white wine
30ml/ 2 tbsp chopped fresh parsley, to garnish

SERVES 6

I Slice the chillies in half, taking care to remove and discard all the seeds. Chop the chillies and the tomatoes roughly and place together in a bowl. Heat the oil in a heavy-based saucepan. Add the garlic and shallots and fry over a low heat for 5 minutes or until the shallots have softened. Stir in the tomatoes and chillies and simmer for 10 minutes.

2 Scrub the mussels carefully, pull off the beards and discard any which are open. Add with the white wine to the saucepan, then cover tightly and cook over a high heat for about 5 minutes or until almost all the mussels have opened. Discard any mussels that remain closed. Spoon the mussels into a large bowl, scatter the parsley over the top and serve.

Scallop & Mussel Kebabs

INGREDIENTS

40g/ 1½oz/ 3 tbsp butter, softened
30ml/ 2 tbsp finely chopped fresh parsley, plus
parsley sprigs to garnish
15ml/ 1 tbsp lemon juice
32 queen scallops
24 fresh mussels, scrubbed and bearded
8 bacon rashers
50g/ 2oz/ 1 cup fresh white breadcrumbs
60ml/ 2fl oz/ ¼ cup olive oil
salt and ground black pepper
twists of lemon rind, to garnish
hot toast, to serve

SERVES 8

1 Using a wooden spoon, beat the butter with the parsley in a mixing bowl. Gradually beat in the lemon juice, with salt and pepper to taste. Set aside until required. Open the scallops, reserving their liquid in a small saucepan. Cook the scallops in their liquid (or in a little fish stock or white wine) until they begin to shrink. Drain and pat dry with kitchen paper.

2 Place the mussels in a large pan. Pour in water to a depth of 2.5cm/1in. Cover tightly and cook for 5–8 minutes until the mussels have opened. Discard any that remain closed. Remove the mussels from their shells and pat dry on kitchen paper.

3 You will need eight 15cm/6in metal or wooden skewers. If using wooden skewers, soak them in water for 30 minutes before use. Pierce a rasher of bacon with one of the skewers, then thread four scallops and three mussels alternately on to the skewer, weaving the bacon in between. Thread the remaining skewers in the same way. Preheat the grill.

4 Spread out the breadcrumbs on a plate. Brush the seafood with olive oil and roll in the crumbs to coat all over. Grill for 4–5 minutes on each side, until lightly browned. Serve with the toast and flavoured butter, garnished with parsley and lemon rind twists.

Haddock & Broccoli Chowder

INGREDIENTS

4 spring onions, sliced
450g/1lb potatoes, diced
1 bay leaf
300ml/½ pint/1¼ cups fish stock or water
300ml/½ pint/1¼ cups skimmed milk
675g/1½lb broccoli florets, thawed if frozen
450g/1lb smoked haddock fillets, skinned
200g/7oz can sweetcorn, drained
ground black pepper
chopped spring onions, to garnish
crusty bread, to serve

SERVES 4

28

1 Place the sliced spring onions and diced potatoes in a large saucepan. Add the bay leaf. Pour over the stock or water and skimmed milk. Bring the liquid to the boil, then lower the heat, cover the pan tightly and allow to simmer for 10 minutes.

2 Quarter any large broccoli florets. Cut the haddock into bite-size chunks. Add the broccoli, haddock and sweetcorn to the pan, with a generous grinding of black pepper. Cover the pan and simmer for about 5 minutes or until the fish is cooked through.

3 Remove the bay leaf. Serve the chowder in heated bowls topped with chopped spring onions and ground black pepper. Serve with crusty bread.

Quick Seafood Pizza

INGREDIENTS

450g/1lb/4 cups strong white flour
15ml/1 tbsp sugar
5ml/1 tsp easy-blend dried yeast
5ml/1 tsp sea salt
30ml/2 tbsp olive oil
300ml/½ pint/1¼ cups hand-hot water
TOPPING
15ml/1 tbsp olive oil
1 onion, finely chopped
2 x 400g/14oz cans chopped tomatoes
15ml/1 tbsp chopped fresh thyme
8 canned sardines
115g/4oz cooked prawns, peeled
and deveined
8 cherry tomatoes, halved
thyme sprigs, to garnish

SERVES 4

1 Sift the flour into a large bowl. Stir in the sugar, yeast and salt. Add the olive oil and water and mix to a firm dough. Knead on a lightly floured surface for about 10 minutes, until the dough is smooth, elastic and no longer sticky. Return it to the cleaned bowl, cover and leave in a warm place until the dough has doubled in bulk.

2 Make the topping. Heat the oil and fry the onion over a low heat for 8–10 minutes, until softened.

3 Stir in the chopped tomatoes and thyme, with plenty of salt and pepper to taste. Simmer, stirring occasionally, for 15 minutes.

4 Preheat the oven to 200°C/400°F/Gas 6. Knock back the dough, knead it for 5 minutes, then cut it into four equal pieces. Roll each piece out to a round, about 20cm/8in in diameter. Place the rounds on baking sheets.

5 Spread each dough round generously with the tomato sauce and top with the sardines, prawns and cherry tomatoes. Bake for 20 minutes until the crust is golden and crisp. Garnish the pizzas with thyme sprigs and serve.

Grilled Snapper with Hot Mango Salsa

INGREDIENTS

350g/12oz new potatoes
3 eggs
115g/4oz French beans, topped,
tailed and halved
4 red snapper, about 350g/12oz each, cleaned
and trimmed
30ml/2 tbsp olive oil
175g/6oz mixed lettuce leaves
2 cherry tomatoes
salt and ground black pepper
SALSA
1 ripe mango, about 175g/6oz
45ml/3 tbsp chopped fresh coriander
½ red chilli, seeded and chopped
2.5cm/1in fresh root ginger, grated
juice of 2 limes
generous pinch of celery salt

SERVES 4

1 Place the potatoes in a large saucepan of salted water. Bring to the boil then lower the heat and simmer for 15–20 minutes or until just tender. Drain.

2 Bring a second pan of salted water to the boil. Boil the eggs for 4 minutes, then add the beans and cook for 6 minutes more, so that the eggs have had a total of 10 minutes. Remove the eggs and place in a bowl of cold water. Drain the beans, refresh under cold running water and drain. When the eggs are cold, shell them and cut into quarters.

3 Make the salsa by processing all the ingredients in a food processor or blender until smooth. Add salt and pepper to taste and set aside. Preheat the grill to

moderate. Slash each snapper three times on either side, place on the grill rack and brush with olive oil. Grill for 12 minutes, turning once.

4 Meanwhile strew the lettuce leaves on four individual plates. Cut the new potatoes and tomatoes in half, and arrange them around the rim of each plate, with the beans and hard-boiled eggs. Centre a grilled snapper on each salad and serve at once, with the salsa.

Salads

Spinach Salad with Bacon & Prawns

INGREDIENTS

115g/4oz fresh young spinach leaves
½ head oak leaf lettuce, roughly torn
30ml/2 tbsp sherry vinegar
2 garlic cloves, finely chopped
5ml/1 tsp Dijon mustard
90ml/6 tbsp olive oil
115g/4oz rindless streaky bacon rashers,
cut into strips
12 cooked Mediterranean prawns,
shelled and deveined
salt and ground black pepper
crusty bread, to serve

SERVES 4

1 Arrange all the spinach and oak leaf lettuce leaves neatly on four individual serving plates. Gently heat the vinegar, garlic, mustard and olive oil in a saucepan. Whisk until slightly thickened and add salt and pepper to taste. Set aside and keep hot.

2 Gently fry the bacon until the fat runs, then raise the heat and cook until golden and crisp.

3 Add the Mediterranean prawns to the fried bacon and toss over the heat for a few minutes until they are warmed right through.

4 Spoon the bacon and prawns on to the lettuce leaves. Add the dressing to the frying pan and scrape the bottom of the pan with a wooden spoon to incorporate any bacon bits. Pour a little of the hot dressing over each salad and serve at once with crusty bread.

Warm Salmon Salad

INGREDIENTS

175g/6oz mixed salad leaves (see Cook's Tip)
115g/4oz fine green beans, topped and tailed
45ml/3 tbsp groundnut oil
450g/1lb salmon fillet, skinned and cut into
bite-size pieces
15ml/1 tbsp toasted sesame seeds
DRESSING
grated rind of ½ orange
juice of 1 orange
5ml/1 tsp Dijon mustard
15ml/1 tbsp chopped fresh tarragon
30ml/2 tbsp sesame oil
salt and ground black pepper

SERVES 4

2 Bring a saucepan of salted water to the boil, add the beans and cook for 5–6 minutes. Meanwhile heat the groundnut oil in a frying pan. Fry the salmon pieces for 3–4 minutes until lightly browned. Pour the dressing over the salmon in the pan and toss gently over the heat for 30 seconds. Remove the pan from the heat.

3 Drain the green beans in a sieve and arrange them on top of the mixed salad leaves. Spoon the pieces of salmon, together with the hot tarragon and mustard dressing, over the salad. Sprinkle each plate with some sesame seeds and serve at once.

1 Divide all of the mixed salad leaves among four individual serving plates or bowls. To make the salad dressing, mix the orange rind and juice, Dijon mustard and chopped tarragon together in a small bowl. Whisk in the sesame oil and add salt and ground black pepper to taste. Whisk again until all the dressing ingredients are fully combined.

COOK'S TIP

When time is short, buy a packet of mixed salad leaves from the supermarket. Alternatively, put together your own selection, choosing from young spinach leaves, rocket, radicchio, frisée and oak leaf lettuce. Just toss the leaves together.

Melon & Crabmeat Salad

INGREDIENTS

450g/1lb fresh crabmeat
1½ melons (cantaloupe or small honeydew)
120ml/4fl oz/½ cup mayonnaise
60ml/4 tbsp soured cream or natural yogurt
30ml/2 tbsp olive oil
30ml/2 tbsp fresh lemon or lime juice
3 spring onions, finely chopped
30ml/2 tbsp chopped fresh coriander
1.25ml/¼ tsp cayenne pepper
3 heads of chicory, trimmed and separated
into leaves
salt and ground black pepper
coriander sprigs, to garnish

SERVES 6

1 Pick over the crabmeat, removing any shell or cartilage and discarding it. Try to keep the pieces of crabmeat as large as you possibly can. Using a sharp knife, cut the whole melon in half on a chopping board. Spoon out the seeds from the melon halves and discard, then cut the melon into thin slices and remove the skin.

2 Mix the mayonnaise and soured cream or natural yogurt in a mixing bowl. Beat in the oil and lemon or lime juice and add the spring onions, chopped coriander and cayenne, mixing until all the ingredients are well combined. Carefully fold in the crabmeat.

3 Arrange the chicory leaves and melon slices on plates. Spoon a mound of the dressed crabmeat on to each plate and garnish with coriander sprigs.

Tuna & Bean Salad

INGREDIENTS

2 x 400g/14oz cans cannellini or
borlotti beans
2 x 200g/7oz cans tuna, drained
30ml/2 tbsp lemon juice
15ml/1 tbsp chopped fresh parsley
60ml/4 tbsp extra virgin olive oil
3 spring onions, thinly sliced
salt and ground black pepper
flat leaf parsley sprig, to garnish

SERVES 4–6

3 Whisk together the lemon juice and chopped parsley in a mixing bowl using a small spoon or whisk. Gradually pour in the olive oil, with salt and pepper to taste, whisking all the time until all the ingredients are combined. Pour the dressing over the tuna and beans and sprinkle with the spring onions. Garnish with the parsley sprig and serve.

1 Drain beans in a large sieve or colander. Rinse under cold water and drain again to remove the excess liquid. Stand the sieve or colander over a bowl and leave for a few minutes, shaking it occasionally, until all the liquid has drained away.

2 Once the beans are as dry as possible, tip them into a serving dish or spread them on a large serving plate. Break the drained tuna into fairly large flakes and arrange over the beans.

Provençal Salad

INGREDIENTS

225g/8oz French beans
*450g/1lb new potatoes, peeled and cut
into 2.5cm/1in cubes*
*1 small cos or round lettuce, torn into
bite-size pieces*
4 plum tomatoes, quartered
1 small cucumber, peeled, seeded and diced
1 green or red pepper, thinly sliced
4 hard-boiled eggs, quartered
24 black olives
*225g/8oz can tuna in brine,
drained and flaked*
*50g/2oz can anchovy fillets in olive oil,
drained and torn in half*
salt and ground black pepper
basil leaves, to garnish
ANCHOVY VINAIGRETTE
20ml/4 tsp Dijon mustard
50g/2oz can anchovy fillets in olive oil, drained
1 garlic clove, crushed
60ml/4tbsp lemon juice or white wine vinegar
120ml/4fl oz/½ cup sunflower oil
120ml/4fl oz/½ cup extra virgin olive oil

SERVES 4–6

1 To make the anchovy vinaigrette, combine the mustard, anchovies and garlic in a bowl or mortar. Mix to a paste by pressing the ingredients against the side of the bowl with a fork or pestle. Season generously with pepper, then whisk in the sunflower oil, then the olive oil, in a steady stream. Whisk until the dressing is smooth and creamy.

2 Bring a saucepan of lightly salted water to the boil, add the beans and cook for 3 minutes until just tender. Using a slotted spoon, transfer the beans to a colander. Refresh them under cold running water and drain again.

3 Add the cubed potatoes to the pan of boiling water, lower the heat and simmer for 10–15 minutes until they are just tender. Drain them thoroughly  and tip into a mixing bowl. Sprinkle with a spoonful of the anchovy vinaigrette.

4 Arrange the lettuce, tomatoes, cucumber, and pepper on a platter. Add the French beans and potatoes, then arrange the eggs, olives, tuna and anchovies on top. Drizzle with the remaining vinaigrette and serve garnished with basil.

Mixed Seafood Salad

INGREDIENTS

1 small onion, quartered
1 bay leaf
350g/12oz prepared small squid
200g/7oz raw prawns, in the shell
*750g/1½lb fresh mussels, scrubbed
and bearded*
450g/1lb fresh small clams, scrubbed
175ml/6fl oz/¾ cup white wine
1 fennel bulb
45ml/3 tbsp lemon juice
1 garlic clove, crushed
75ml/5 tbsp extra virgin olive oil
salt and ground black pepper

SERVES 6–8

1 Put the onion and bay leaf in a pan of water. Bring to the boil, drop in the squid and cook for about 10 minutes. Remove the squid and slice them into 1cm/½in rings. Cut each tentacle section in two.

2 Put the prawns in the pan of boiling water and cook for 2 minutes or until they turn pink. Drain and reserve the cooking liquid as the basis for a fish soup, if liked. Rinse the mussels and clams in several changes of cold water and discard any open shells which do not close when tapped. Place in a large saucepan with the wine. Cover the pan tightly and cook for 5–8 minutes until most of the shells have opened. Discard any that remain closed. Remove the shellfish with a slotted spoon.

3 Using a small spoon, remove all the clams from their shells and place in a large serving bowl. Remove the mussels from their shells and add them to the bowl. Set the fennel fronds aside, then chop the bulb into bite-size pieces. Add to the bowl with the squid and prawns.

4 Make a dressing by combining the lemon juice and garlic in a small bowl. Whisk in the olive oil, with salt and pepper to taste. Chop some of the fennel fronds finely and add them to the dressing. Stir, then pour the dressing over the seafood. Garnish with the remaining fennel fronds. Serve at room temperature or lightly chilled.

40

Mid-week Meals

Moroccan Fish Tagine

INGREDIENTS

2 garlic cloves, crushed
30ml/2 tbsp ground cumin
30ml/2 tbsp paprika
1 small red chilli, seeded and finely chopped
30ml/2 tbsp tomato purée
60ml/4 tbsp lemon juice
4 whiting or cod fillets, about 175g/6oz each
350g/12oz tomatoes, sliced
2 green peppers, seeded and thinly sliced
salt and ground black pepper
chopped fresh coriander or parsley, to garnish
broccoli, to serve

SERVES 4

1 In a small bowl, mix the garlic, cumin, paprika, red chilli, tomato purée and lemon juice together to form a paste. Arrange the fish in a single layer on a shallow dish and generously spread the spicy garlic paste over it, using a spoon. Cover and chill for about 30 minutes to allow the flavours of the paste to penetrate the fish. Preheat the oven to 200°C/400°F/Gas 6.

2 Arrange half the tomato and pepper slices in a baking dish large enough to hold all of the fish in a single layer. Arrange the fish on top and cover with the rest of the tomato and pepper slices. Sprinkle with salt and pepper. Cover the dish with foil and bake for about 45 minutes, or until the fish is tender. Sprinkle with chopped coriander or parsley and serve at once, with lightly cooked broccoli.

Halibut with Fresh Tomato & Basil Salsa

INGREDIENTS

4 halibut fillets, about 175g/6oz each
45ml/3 tbsp olive oil
basil leaves, to garnish
BASIL SALSA
1 tomato, roughly chopped
¼ red onion, finely chopped
1 small jalapeno pepper, chopped
30ml/2 tbsp balsamic vinegar
10 large basil leaves, plus extra to garnish
15ml/1 tbsp olive oil
salt and ground black pepper

SERVES 4

44

1 Make the salsa. Mix the tomato, onion, jalapeno pepper and vinegar together in a small bowl. Tear the basil leaves into shreds. Stir them into the salsa with the olive oil. Add salt and pepper to taste and mix together well. Cover and leave to marinate in a cool place for at least 3 hours.

2 Preheat the grill. Brush the halibut fillets generously with olive oil, season with salt and plenty of black pepper and place on a wire rack over the grill pan. Cook for about 4 minutes on each side, depending on thickness. Baste the fish with olive oil as necessary. It is cooked when it flakes easily when tested with the tip of a sharp knife. Serve at once, with the salsa, garnished with basil leaves.

Cod & Spinach Parcels

INGREDIENTS

4 pieces of thick cod fillet, about 175g/6oz
each, skinned
225g/8oz large spinach leaves
2.5ml/½ tsp grated nutmeg
45ml/3 tbsp white wine
salt and ground black pepper
chopped fresh parsley and lemon wedges,
to garnish

SERVES 4

1 Preheat the oven to 180°C/350°F/ Gas 4. Season the fish well with salt and ground black pepper. Bring a large saucepan of water to the boil, add the spinach leaves and blanch for 1 minute. Drain, refresh under cold running water and drain again.

2 Pat the spinach leaves dry on kitchen paper, then use them to wrap each piece of fish. Sprinkle with nutmeg. Place in a roasting tin, pour over the wine and bake for 15 minutes. Slice the fish and serve at once, garnished with the parsley and lemon wedges.

Prawn Creole

INGREDIENTS

75g/3oz/6 tbsp butter
1 large onion, halved and thinly sliced
1 green pepper, halved, seeded and thinly sliced
2 celery sticks, thinly sliced
2 garlic cloves, thinly sliced
1 bay leaf
30ml/2 tbsp paprika
450g/1lb tomatoes, peeled and chopped
250ml/8fl oz/1 cup tomato juice
20ml/4 tsp Worcestershire sauce
4-6 dashes of Tabasco sauce
pinch of salt
25ml/1½ tbsp cornflour
75ml/5 tbsp water
*chopped fresh parsley and shreds of lemon
rind, to garnish*
1.5kg/3lb raw prawns, peeled and deveined
boiled rice, to serve

SERVES 6–8

1 Melt 25g/1oz/2 tbsp of the butter in a wide pan. Sauté the onion, green pepper, celery, garlic and bay leaf for 1–2 minutes. Add the paprika, tomatoes and tomato juice, then stir in the sauces. Bring to the boil, lower the heat and simmer, uncovered, until the mixture has reduced by about a quarter, by which time the vegetables should have softened. Season with salt.

2 Mix the cornflour with the water and add to the tomato sauce. Heat, stirring constantly, until it thickens. Turn the heat down to its lowest setting.

3 Meanwhile melt the remaining butter in a frying pan. Sauté the prawns, in batches if necessary, for about 2–4 minutes or until pink and tender. When they are all cooked, add them to the sauce. Stir over the heat for about 30 seconds. Check the seasoning.

4 Spoon the rice on to one side of a serving dish, scatter the parsley and lemon rind over the top, and fill the remaining space with the prawn mixture. Serve at once.

46

Spanish Seafood Paella

INGREDIENTS

3 prepared baby squid
225g/8oz monkfish or cod fillet, skinned
1 red mullet, filleted and skinned (optional)
60ml/4 tbsp olive oil
1 onion, chopped
3 garlic cloves, finely chopped
1 red pepper, seeded and sliced
4 tomatoes, peeled and chopped
225g/8oz/1¼ cups arborio rice
475ml/16fl oz/2 cups fish stock
150ml/¼ pint/⅔ cup white wine
75g/3oz/½ cup frozen peas
4-5 saffron strands soaked in 30ml/2 tbsp
hot water
115g/4oz cooked prawns, peeled and deveined
8 fresh mussels, scrubbed and bearded
15ml/1 tbsp chopped fresh parsley (optional)
salt and ground black pepper
lemon halves or wedges, to serve

SERVES 4

1 Cut the body of each squid into rings; chop the tentacles. Cut the monkfish or cod into chunks and do the same with the red mullet, if using. Heat 30ml/2 tbsp of the oil in a paella pan or large deep frying pan, add the squid and fish and stir-fry for 2 minutes. Tip the contents of the pan into a bowl and set aside.

2 Heat the remaining oil in the pan. Add the onion, garlic and pepper. Fry for 6–7 minutes. Stir in the tomatoes and fry for 2 minutes, then add the rice and stir to coat the grains with oil. Cook for 2–3 minutes. Add the fish stock, wine, peas and saffron liquid. Season generously and mix.

3 Gently stir in the reserved par-cooked squid and fish. Add the prawns, then push the mussels into the rice. Cover tightly and cook over a gentle heat for about 30 minutes, or until the stock has been absorbed but the mixture is still moist.

4 Keeping the pan tightly closed, remove it from the heat and leave it to stand for 5 minutes. Check that all the mussels have opened (discard any that remain closed), sprinkle the paella with the parsley, if using, and serve with lemon halves or wedges.

Smoked Trout Pilaff

INGREDIENTS

225g/ 8oz/ 1¼ cups basmati rice
40g/ 1½oz/ 3 tbsp butter
2 onions, sliced into rings
1 garlic clove, crushed
2 bay leaves
2 whole cloves
2 green cardamom pods
2 cinnamon sticks
5ml/ 1 tsp cumin seeds
4 smoked trout fillets, skinned
50g/ 2oz/ ½ cup slivered almonds, toasted
50g/ 2oz/ ⅓ cup seedless raisins
30ml/ 2 tbsp chopped fresh parsley, plus a few
extra leaves to garnish
salt
mango chutney and poppadums, to serve

SERVES 4

1 Wash the rice thoroughly in several changes of water. Drain well. Set aside. Melt the butter in a large frying pan and fry the onion until well browned, stirring frequently. Add the garlic, bay leaves and spices. Stir-fry for 1 minute.

2 Stir the rice into the onion, then add 600ml/ 1 pint/2½ cups boiling salted water. Bring to the boil, cover the pan tightly and reduce the heat to low. Cook the rice for 20–25 minutes until tender.

3 Flake all of the smoked trout and add it to the pan with the almonds, raisins and chopped parsley. Fork through gently, then cover the pan again and allow the smoked trout to warm through for a few minutes. Serve at once, garnished with the parsley leaves and accompanied by mango chutney and poppadums.

49

Mediterranean Plaice Rolls

INGREDIENTS

75g/ 3oz/ 6 tbsp butter
4 plaice fillets, about 225g/ 8oz each, skinned
1 small onion, chopped
1 celery stick, thinly sliced
115g/ 4oz/ 2 cups fresh white breadcrumbs
3-4 drained sun-dried tomatoes in oil, chopped
*45ml/ 3 tbsp chopped fresh parsley, plus extra
to garnish*
30ml/ 2 tbsp pine nuts, toasted
*50g/ 2oz can anchovy fillets, drained
and chopped*
75ml/ 5 tbsp fish stock
ground black pepper

SERVES 4

1 Preheat the oven to 180°C/350°F/Gas 4. Grease a baking dish with a little of the butter. Cut the plaice fillets in half lengthways to make eight smaller fillets. Melt the remaining butter in a frying pan and cook the onion and celery over a low heat for 15 minutes until softened but not coloured.

2 With a wooden spoon, mix the breadcrumbs, sundried tomatoes, parsley, pine nuts, and anchovies together in a large mixing bowl. Stir in the softened vegetables with the pan juices. Mix together until combined. Season with pepper.

3 Divide the stuffing into eight equal portions and roll each one into a ball. Place each stuffing ball at one end of a plaice fillet and roll up. Secure the rolls with individual cocktail sticks.

4 Arrange all the plaice rolls in the prepared baking dish. Pour over the stock and cover the dish with a piece of buttered foil. Bake for about 20 minutes or until the fish flakes easily when tested with the point of a sharp knife. Remove all of the cocktail sticks and sprinkle the fish with chopped parsley. When serving the plaice rolls, drizzle a little of the cooking juices over each portion.

50

Mackerel Kebabs with Parsley Dressing

INGREDIENTS

450g/ 1lb mackerel fillets
finely grated rind and juice of 1 lemon
45ml/ 3 tbsp chopped fresh parsley
16 cherry tomatoes
8 pitted black olives
salt and ground black pepper
chopped fresh parsley, to garnish
mixed salad leaves (optional) and
boiled rice or noodles, to serve

SERVES 4

52

1 Cut the fish into 4cm/1½in chunks and place in a bowl. Add half the lemon rind and juice, half the parsley and a sprinkling of salt and pepper. Stir to mix, then cover the bowl and leave in a cool place to marinate for 30 minutes. Preheat the grill.

2 You will need eight 15cm/6in metal or wooden skewers. If using wooden skewers, soak them in water for 30 minutes before use. Drain the fish, discard the marinade, and thread the chunks alternately with the tomatoes and olives on the skewers. Grill the kebabs for 3–4 minutes, turning occasionally, until the fish is cooked through.

3 In a bowl, mix the remaining lemon rind and juice with the rest of the parsley. Add salt and pepper to taste. Serve the kebabs on a bed of rice or noodles, drizzle with the dressing and sprinkle with chopped parsley. Add a salad garnish, if liked.

Golden Fish Pie

INGREDIENTS

675g/ 1½lb white fish fillets
300ml/ ½ pint/ 1¼ cups milk
1 bay leaf
5ml/ 1 tsp black peppercorns
½ onion, sliced
115g/ 4oz cooked prawns, peeled and deveined
115g/ 4oz/ ½ cup butter
50g/ 2oz/ ½ cup plain flour
300ml/ ½ pint/ 1¼ cups single cream
75g/ 3oz Gruyère cheese, grated
1 bunch watercress, leaves stripped from
stems, chopped
5ml/ 1 tsp Dijon mustard
5 sheets filo pastry
salt and ground black pepper

SERVES 4–6

1 Place the fish fillets in a large saucepan. Pour over the milk and add the bay leaf, peppercorns and onion slices. Bring to the boil, lower the heat, cover and simmer for 10–12 minutes, until the fish is almost tender. Do not allow it to overcook.

2 Drain the fish, reserving the milk. Remove the skin and bones, then roughly flake into a shallow pie dish. Scatter the prawns over the top.

3 Melt 50g/2oz/¼ cup of the butter in a pan. Stir in the flour and cook for about 1 minute, then stir in the reserved milk and cream. Bring to the boil, stirring constantly, then lower the heat and simmer for 2–3 minutes, until the sauce thickens.

4 Remove the pan from the heat and stir in the Gruyère, watercress and mustard, with salt and pepper to taste. Pour over the fish and leave to cool.

5 Preheat the oven to 190°C/375°F/Gas 5. Melt the remaining butter. Brush one sheet of the filo pastry with a little of the butter, then crumple up loosely and place on top of the filling. Repeat with the rest of the filo and butter, to cover the fish. Bake for 25–30 minutes, until crisp and golden.

Dinner
Party Dishes

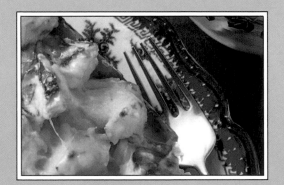

Scottish Salmon with Herb Butter

INGREDIENTS

50g/ 2oz/ ¼ cup butter, softened
finely grated rind of ½ small lemon
15ml/ 1 tbsp lemon juice
15ml/ 1 tbsp chopped fresh dill
4 salmon steaks
2 lemon slices, halved
4 dill sprigs
salt and ground black pepper
new potatoes and salad, to serve

SERVES 4

3 Cut the frozen butter into eight rounds. Place two rounds in the centre of each salmon steak, with half a lemon slice and a dill sprig on top. Close up the foil neatly around the salmon pieces, making sure each parcel is well sealed.

4 Bake the salmon for 20 minutes. Test by partially opening a parcel and piercing the salmon with a sharp knife; the flesh should flake easily. Serve the parcels with new potatoes and salad.

1 Mix together the butter, lemon rind and juice. Add the dill, with seasoning to taste, and mix well. Spoon on to a piece of grease-proof paper and roll up, smoothing with your hands to make a sausage shape. Twist the ends tightly, wrap in clear film and freeze the package for 20 minutes, or until firm.

2 Preheat the oven to 190°C/375°F/Gas 5. Cut out four squares of foil, each large enough to enclose a salmon steak. Grease the squares lightly and centre a salmon steak on each one.

55

Spanish-style Hake

INGREDIENTS

30ml/ 2 tbsp olive oil
25g/ 1oz/ 2 tbsp butter
1 onion, chopped
3 garlic cloves, crushed
15ml/ 1 tbsp plain flour
2.5ml/ ½ tsp paprika
4 hake, cod or haddock cutlets,
about 175g/ 6oz each
225g/ 8oz fine green beans, topped, tailed
and cut into 2.5cm/ 1in lengths
350ml/ 12fl oz/ 1½ cups fish stock
150ml/ ¼ pint/ ⅔ cup dry white wine
30ml/ 2 tbsp dry sherry
16-20 fresh mussels, scrubbed and bearded
45ml/ 3 tbsp chopped fresh parsley
salt and ground black pepper
crusty bread, to serve

SERVES 4

1 Heat the oil and butter in a large frying pan. Add the onion and cook for 5 minutes over a moderate heat, until softened but not browned. Stir in the crushed garlic and cook for 1 minute more.

2 Mix the flour and paprika in a shallow bowl. Lightly dust the fish cutlets with the mixture. Push the onion and garlic to one side of the frying pan, add the fish and fry until golden on both sides.

3 Stir in the beans, stock, wine and sherry. Season, then bring to the boil and cook for 2 minutes.

4 Add the mussels and parsley to the pan, cover tightly and cook for 5–8 minutes or until the mussels have opened. Discard any that remain closed. Divide  among heated shallow soup bowls, sprinkle with pepper, and serve with plenty of crusty bread.

Trout with Hazelnuts

INGREDIENTS

50g/ 2oz/ ½ cup hazelnuts
65g/ 2½oz/ 5 tbsp butter
4 trout, about 275g/ 10oz each
30ml/ 2 tbsp lemon juice
salt and ground black pepper
2 lemon slices, quartered, and flat leaf parsley
sprigs, to garnish

SERVES 4

1 Preheat the grill. Spread out the nuts in a single layer in a grill pan. Toast the nuts, shaking the pan frequently, until the skins split. Tip the nuts on to a clean dish-towel and rub off the skins. Leave the nuts to cool, then chop them coarsely.

2 Heat 50g/2oz/ ¼ cup of the butter in a large frying pan. Season the trout inside and out, and then fry, in batches if necessary, for about 12–15 minutes, turning once, until the skins are brown and the flesh flakes easily when tested with the point of a sharp knife. Drain on kitchen paper, then transfer to a platter and keep hot.

3 Melt the rest of the butter in the frying pan and fry the hazelnuts until evenly browned. With a wooden spoon, stir the lemon juice into the pan and mix

well, then quickly pour the buttery hazelnut sauce over the trout. Serve the trout at once, garnished with the lemon and parsley sprigs.

57

Monkfish, Salmon & Sole Mousseline

INGREDIENTS

225g/8oz monkfish, removed from the bone
225g/8oz sole fillets
2 egg whites
2.5ml/½ tsp grated nutmeg
250ml/8fl oz/1 cup double cream
8 large spinach leaves
350g/12oz salmon fillet
450g/1lb tomatoes
salt and ground black pepper
dill sprigs, to garnish

SERVES 4

1 Line four small ramekins with greaseproof paper. Remove the membrane from the monkfish, if necessary, by cutting it away with a sharp knife and pulling it off. Cut the monkfish into large cubes and place in a food processor or blender. Skin the sole fillets and chop into several large pieces, removing any stray bones. Add to the monkfish, with the egg whites, and process until the mixture is smooth and firm. Scrape into a mixing bowl and chill for 10 minutes.

2 Stir the nutmeg into the mixture and season. Place the bowl over a second bowl filled with ice. Gradually beat in the cream, then chill the mousseline for 30 minutes, by which time it should be thick and firm enough to hold its own shape.

3 Preheat the oven to 180°C/350°F/ Gas 4. Blanch the spinach leaves very briefly in boiling water, then drain and refresh under cold water and drain again. Cut

the salmon into eight slices. Line the base of each ramekin with a slice of salmon, top with a spinach leaf, cut to fit, then add a layer of the mousseline and another spinach leaf. Spoon more mousseline on top and finish with a layer of salmon. Cover each ramekin with a round of greaseproof paper.

4 Place the ramekins in a large roasting tin, pour in boiling water to come halfway up the ramekins and bake for 20 minutes. Meanwhile make the sauce. Grill the tomatoes until the skins are blackened. Scrape the flesh into a food processor or blender, add plenty of salt and pepper, and process to a purée. Invert the fish and mousseline moulds on individual dishes, garnish with dill and serve with the tomato sauce.

Tuna with Pan-fried Tomatoes

INGREDIENTS

4 tuna steaks, about 175g/6oz each
50g/2oz can anchovy fillets, drained
and chopped
3 garlic cloves, chopped
175ml/6fl oz/¾ cup olive oil
60ml/4 tbsp lemon juice
7.5ml/1½ tsp chopped fresh thyme
350g/12oz plum tomatoes, halved
45ml/3 tbsp chopped fresh parsley
8-12 black olives, pitted and chopped
ground black pepper
crusty bread, to serve

SERVES 4

1 Place the tuna steaks in a shallow non-metallic dish which is just large enough to hold them side by side. Place the anchovy fillets and garlic in a mixing bowl, then stir in 60ml/4 tbsp of the oil. Add the lemon juice, thyme and a generous grinding of black pepper. Mix well, pour the mixture over the tuna, cover and leave to marinate for at least 1 hour.

2 Preheat the grill. Drain the tuna, reserving the marinade, and place on the grill rack. Grill for about 4 minutes on each side, basting frequently with the reserved marinade. The tuna steaks should not be overcooked and are ready when the flesh feels firm to the touch.

3 Meanwhile heat the remaining oil in a frying pan. Add the tomatoes and fry for 2 minutes only on each side. Divide the tomatoes between four heated serving plates and scatter over the chopped parsley and olives. Top each portion with a tuna steak.

4 Add the remaining marinade to the pan juices and heat through. Pour over the tomatoes and tuna steaks and serve at once, with crusty bread for mopping up the juices.

Pan-fried Sole

INGREDIENTS

4 Dover sole or lemon sole fillets,
about 675g/ 1½lb, skinned
175ml/ 6fl oz/ ¾ cup milk
75g/ 3oz/ ¾ cup plain flour
30ml/ 2 tbsp corn oil
25g/ 1oz/ 2 tbsp butter
30ml/ 2 tbsp chopped fresh parsley
salt and ground black pepper
lemon wedges, to serve

SERVES 4

1 Rinse the Dover or lemon sole fillets and pat them dry with kitchen paper. Pour the milk into a shallow baking dish, large enough to hold a fish fillet. Spread out the flour in a second shallow dish and season it lightly with salt and pepper.

2 Heat the oil and butter in a large frying pan (big enough to hold two fillets without breaking them) over a moderately high heat. Dip each fish fillet in milk, then in flour, turning until well coated. Shake off the excess flour.

3 Add two fish fillets to the hot oil in the frying pan. Reduce the heat slightly and cook the fish fillets for 3–4 minutes, or until lightly browned, turning once. Remove and keep hot while cooking the remaining fish fillets. Sprinkle the fish with chopped parsley and serve with lemon wedges.

61

Lobster Thermidor

INGREDIENTS

2 live lobsters, about 675g/1½lb each
20g/¾oz/1½ tbsp butter
30ml/2 tbsp plain flour
30ml/2 tbsp brandy
120ml/4fl oz/½ cup milk
90ml/6 tbsp whipping cream
15ml/1 tbsp Dijon mustard
lemon juice (see method)
grated Parmesan cheese, for sprinkling
salt and white pepper
parsley and dill sprigs, to garnish
French bread, to serve

SERVES 2–4

1 Bring a large saucepan of salted water to the boil. Put the lobsters in head first, cover, and cook them for 8–10 minutes or until bright pink. Remove from the pan and cut in half lengthways. Discard the dark sac behind the eyes, then pull out the string-like intestine from the tail. Remove the meat from the shells, reserving the coral and liver, rinse the shells and wipe dry. Cut the meat into bite-size pieces.

2 Melt the butter in a heavy-based saucepan. Stir in the flour and cook for 1 minute, then pour in the brandy and milk, whisking constantly until smooth. Whisk in the cream and mustard.

3 Press the lobster coral and liver through a sieve into the sauce. Whisk very well. Reduce the heat to low and simmer the sauce gently for about 10 minutes, stirring frequently, until it thickens. Stir in lemon juice and seasoning to taste (it may not be necessary to add salt).

4 Preheat the grill. Arrange the lobster shells in a shallow flameproof baking dish. Stir the lobster meat into the sauce and divide the mixture evenly between the shells. Sprinkle lightly with Parmesan and grill until golden. Garnish with parsley and dill and serve at once with French bread.

Index